"*Acha Bacha* shows that a theatre space is not only for white comfort. And Bilal understands and proves this. The writing takes me through the journey of unpacking trauma, homophobia, binary-ness among south asian communities. And still, there is hope. Bilal's achievement here is not just one person's success, it's all of our success."
—Angel Glady

"There are no neat narratives in *Acha Bacha*—the work, like Bilal himself, resists the urge to make things neat, resists the urge for stories of south asians in canada to be models (the minority kind). Precisely because this is a queer and trans story, it cannot be neat. It finds its place, like Bilal does, in an archive we are building, a part of the legacy of cultural production by the brilliant Black and brown queer and trans folks of toronto-ish places. I hope we may all take up the beauty of a million paused moments between brown immigrant mother and child, clasp tightly to the ponderings of the conversations that almost happened, and then steady ourselves when they do. I hope we may breathe deeply when we see the nuances of care between lovers, not the slow sigh of witnessing romance, but the punctuating breathing of knowing that there are truer ways of portraying care, ways that we see here. I cannot recommend enough that you take the time to read and feel your way through this work. It will change you."
—Anu Radha Varma

"*Acha Bacha*'s storytelling weaves the trauma, joy, grief and community felt by queer south asian, muslim communities. Theatre can often feel alienating for racialized communities—*Acha Bacha*'s weaving of urdu and specific community narratives throughout the play is a refreshing addition to affirm that this play is for us and not the (white) voyeuristic gaze. *Acha Bacha* is hard to watch, and can be triggering, as it doesn't shy away from hard subjects like sexual assault, religion and homophobia; Bilal finds that balance to ensure that *Acha Bacha* isn't trauma porn but rather storytelling to push audiences to further engage with these topics."
—Berkha Gupta

D1590051

"What does it feel like to see yourself represented on stage? Baig takes an everyday queer Desi experience and weaves in multidimensional characters to give us permission to feel, love, loathe, be—and every affect in between. At a time when Brownness continues to be underrepresented and understudied, Baig's work queers that space in a way that begins a necessary and critical conversation about intergenerational relationships and their inheritances. This is a gift!"
—Dirk J. Rodricks

"Salim made my life. I loved seeing the way they dressed as an AMAB brown femme/gender expansive person (I wanted part of an outfit), and the way their body was inhabited by gentleness as they moved about the stage. Mirroring the reality of femme folks in relationships with cis men, Salim patiently nurtures their partner Zaya while he struggles, but playwright Bilal Baig ensures this isn't a story where Salim's needs are irrelevant."
—Harris I. Qureshi

"*Acha Bacha* sent me back in time to when I was a young queer Muslim struggling to live under conditions where I was chained from everything, but being tempted by the same hands that chained me. It's a story that is far too common in the Muslim community and a story that needs to be told. Bilal has opened the doors for many more queer Muslims to come forward and tell their stories with this play."
—Humza A. Mian

"Bilal Baig's *Acha Bacha* is a refreshing artistic intervention—written by and for the people it represents in a spirit of love and compassion, it refuses the typical Orientalist framing applied to art about Brown/Muslim communities. More than anything, the play offers south asian Muslims what we are so often denied—the privilege of complexity, to be more than "good" or "bad," but to be both and neither. That is, it depicts us in our humanity. *Acha Bacha* is interesting, engaging and pleasurable to experience, making it an effective vehicle for the challenging content it presents. I look forward to more exciting art from Bilal Baig."
—Khadijah Kanji

"*Acha Bacha* is a miraculous, groundbreaking play that takes you on a messy, nuanced journey through the intersections of race, gender, sexuality, Islam, family and the ways we run away from the suburbs, ourselves and how we return. Bilal unapologetically writes the complexities of navigating childhood trauma within this context—something I didn't even know I needed. Nuanced, surprising and necessary!"
—kumari giles

"This a story about love. But not a single page mimics tiring Bollywood tropes. Instead, we see the gendered dynamics of a Muslim family and, by extension, the demands on all of our masculinities to conform to painful norms. Baig shares a story about queer love that isn't given a fair chance when lovers and mothers choose denial and self-preservation over the multiple truths that are staring right at them. While many would rather do away with a subplot of sexual abuse and prefer the tidiness of a simple coming-of-age tale, *Acha Bacha* takes us on a journey that exposes the insides of our community—and this time we can't turn a blind eye."
—Rahim Thawer

"*Acha Bacha* is the kind of storytelling that we need. It was surreal to see my experiences and those of people around me reflected on stage."
—Robbie Ahmed

"Weaving slice-of-life scenes with flashbacks, *Acha Bacha* eloquently portrays a nuanced life that is all too familiar to queer desi Muslim youth growing up in the suburbs as we navigate, negotiate and reconcile our relationships to ourselves and to others. The play, like its playwright, is brilliant, imaginative and puts queer brown people at the forefront. It is a poignant reminder of what happens to us in a world fraught with violence against queer people."
—Saadia Khan

ACHA BACHA

ACHA BACHA

BILAL BAIG

PLAYWRIGHTS CANADA PRESS
TORONTO

LIBRARY AND ARCHIVES CANADA CATALOGUING IN PUBLICATION
Title: Acha bacha / Bilal Baig.
Names: Baig, Bilal, author.
Description: A play.
Identifiers: Canadiana (print) 20200234846 | Canadiana (ebook) 20200234870 | ISBN 9780369100900 (softcover) | ISBN 9780369100917 (PDF) | ISBN 9780369100924 (EPUB) | ISBN 9780369100931 (Kindle)
Classification: LCC PS8603.A44 A74 2020 | DDC C812/.6—dc23

Playwrights Canada Press operates on Mississaugas of the Credit, Wendat, Anishinaabe, Métis, and Haudenosaunee land. It always was and always will be Indigenous land.

We acknowledge the financial support of the Canada Council for the Arts—which last year invested $153 million to bring the arts to Canadians throughout the country—the Ontario Arts Council (OAC), Ontario Creates, and the Government of Canada for our publishing activities.

 Canada Council
for the Arts
Conseil des arts
du Canada

 ONTARIO ARTS COUNCIL
CONSEIL DES ARTS DE L'ONTARIO
an Ontario government agency
un organisme du gouvernement de l'Ontario

 Canadä

 ONTARIO | ONTARIO
CREATES | CRÉATIF

INTRODUCTION BY KAMA LA MACKEREL

When I first encountered Bilal Baig's striking spirit, it was not quite through their playwriting. In 2017 I ran a pilot program in performance creation for trans women and trans femmes in Toronto with the Artists Mentoring Youth (AMY) Project. After I ran the initial project, Bilal took over as Artistic Director of the program, which they continued to develop and expand over the past few years. So I first got to know Bilal as a "people's person"—an arts facilitator who is deeply committed to developing creative and resilient community practices. It is only later that I discovered Bilal's artistic voice: that of an emerging theatre practitioner with a determined vision for their work; someone who has diligently and honestly pondered the place that their work should occupy in relationship to community, theatre readership and audiences, and to the larger structures within which performance operates and circulates.

Entering the literary and theatrical worlds created by Bilal Baig is like stepping into a space that is unapologetic. Baig makes no excuses for their artistic vision: their storytelling is courageous, their characters are truthful and the world view they portray is cosmopolitan, hybrid, complex and unafraid. It is remarkable to bear witness and engage with the work of such a young artistic voice that is at once so strong and nuanced.

Acha Bacha offers a road map to rewrite our contemporary and future societies and the ways in which we relate to each other, particularly when existing in the shadows of unnamed intergenerational trauma emanating from the legacies of displacement and exploitation characteristic of modernity. At the core of this play, Baig asks us to reckon with questions that lie at the heart of relationship building: How do we make space for hurt and love, for rage and forgiveness, within our utmost intimate relationships? How do we make space for each other and find vocabularies for our multiple narratives when our lives are imbricated with love, betrayal, trauma, shame, silence and desire? How can we create spaces of belonging and safety within our intimacies?

Baig's characters are complex in their personhood, in their humanity. Each existing under social relations fraught with power—race, class, gender, ethnicity, sexuality, etc.—as practising Muslims living in the Greater Toronto Area post-9/11, the characters in *Acha Bacha* are beset by contradictions: they are taunted by the workings of memory, they mis/remember and mis/recognize themselves and others. They suffer and try to heal from their hurt but remain stuck in the symptoms of their troubles without being able to get to their source. Through it all, they try to transform themselves, caught between narratives that are immediately available to them and those towards which their imagination is reaching.

Acha Bacha provides us with no easy answer, no redeeming narrative, no cathartic release. Baig holds each of these characters in all of their complexities, making space to honour their multiple truths, the fragmented and often contradictory parts of their internal conflicts, their vulnerabilities and blind spots. Each of the characters tries hard to communicate a coherent narrative of their self within the intimacy of their relationship with each other, and they fail, and they try again. As an audience and a readership, we remain enmeshed in the complexity of feelings that emanates from Baig's work, which is uncomfortable because it is so deeply truthful, so honestly human.

Written in an unapologetic hybrid of English and Urdu, Baig's storytelling challenges the dominating definitions of what it means to be queer, what it means in be Muslim and what it means to be queer and Muslim. While it is not uncommon to expect such narratives to pit Islam against queerness, Eastern beliefs against Western practices, *Acha Bacha* deconstructs this trope and refashions a world where there are multiple ways of being queer, of being Muslim, of being queer Muslims. Baig does not fix any of these identities in definitions; instead, they offer us a cast of characters whose experiences are heterogenous, nuanced, complicated and who express the multiplicity of ways in which one can exist within the intersections of these experiences. In this sense, Baig crafts a theatrical work that challenges the monolithic nature of dominating post/colonial queer narratives.

But more than anything *Acha Bacha* and Baig's body of work offer a cosmopolitan praxis that looks towards the future and expresses what it means to be Canadian while also being queer, Muslim, South Asian, racialized, of the diaspora . . . Baig's literary and performative work enacts a disruption of singular narratives that categorizes and pigeonholes our identities and lived experiences. *Acha Bacha* is a testimony to the messiness of life and the complexity of our interpersonal relationships and reimagines new ways of being, of loving, of recognizing ourselves and each other.

In spite of being an emerging artist, the strength of Bilal Baig's voice is remarkable, one for which we should be watching out and that will likely influence the future of Canadian theatre.

Kama La Mackerel is a Montreal-based Mauritian-Canadian multidisciplinary artist, educator, community-arts facilitator and literary translator who works within and across performance, photography, installations, textiles, digital art and literature. Their art practice is intertextual and intertextural. They have exhibited and performed their work internationally and their writing in English, French and Kreol has appeared in publications both online and in print. Their debut poetry collection ZOM-FAM *was published by Metonymy Press in 2020.*

Here's to you, Babar.
Thank you for letting me cry in your room on that shitty night.
Where would I be without you?

NOTES ON STRUCTURE

When a forward slash (/) appears in a character's speech, it indicates that the next character should speak at that point.

It is intentional that the Urdu written in this play is not translated. It must not be translated in any production of this work as well. However, the use of ASL interpretation to include deaf and/or hard-of-hearing audiences is strongly encouraged when possible. If an interpreter who understands Urdu cannot be found, please contact me for the English translation of this text.

The Urdu is spelled out phonetically in English, so if you don't speak Urdu but are cast in this play, just follow the way the word is spelled and you'll most likely be saying it kind of right. An intention of this work is to feature brown bodies on stage—not only Urdu-speaking brown bodies on stage. I'd also suggest hiring an Urdu dialogue coach . . . just in case.

This play is fluid. I ask that you honour its fluidity in your staging, pacing and in all design choices.

Acha Bacha was first produced by Theatre Passe Muraille and Buddies in Bad Times Theatre at Theatre Passe Muraille, Toronto, from February 1 to 18, 2018, with the following cast and creative team:

Shelly Antony
Qasim Khan
Omar Alex Khan
Matt Nethersole
Ellora Patnaik

Directed by Brendan Healy
Assistant direction by Erum Khan
Set and costume design by Joanna Yu
Assistant costume design by Ann Maisurdze
Lighting design by C.J. Astronomo
Sound design and music by Richard Feren
Stage managed by Kat Chin
Assistant stage management by Christine Luksts
Script coordination by Tijiki Morris

CHARACTERS

Ma (she/her): the mother, early fifties.
Zaya (he/him): the mother's son, late twenties.
Maulana (he/him): the imam, late fifties.
Mubeen (he/him): the imam's son, late twenties.
Salim (they/them): Zaya's genderqueer lover, early thirties.

ZAYA opens his eyes. He looks down. SALIM—in a bra, bangles, makeup and painted nails—is blowing him. He tries to focus but can't. SALIM slows down, then stops.

SALIM: Kya ho gaya?

ZAYA: Uh, nothing I . . .

SALIM: You wanna stop?

ZAYA: No uh wait.

SALIM: Hum stop kar saktey hain.

ZAYA: Just give me a second.

SALIM: Okay. Take your time.

A little silence.

ZAYA: I—I'm just feeling . . .

SALIM: It's okay.

ZAYA: I'm sorry.

3

SALIM: It's okay. Chalo, let's go to bed.

ZAYA: No, Salim, wait. I don't wanna sleep yet. Can we—

SALIM: Pyaare, I really can't watch another episode of *Koffee with Karan*.

ZAYA: I wasn't gonna suggest that. Um. Do you wanna just sit with me for a bit?

SALIM: Are you still high?

ZAYA: No, no, I don't think so. I'm just feeling—weird—so I don't think I'll be able to sleep right away.

SALIM: You want to talk about it? Tum mujhe batha sakthay ho.

ZAYA: Well it's—it doesn't make sense—I just, I feel like if I go to sleep I'm gonna wake up and you won't be here.

SALIM sits close to ZAYA.

SALIM: I'll be here, pyaare. Meh kahin nahi ja rahi hoon . . . yet.

ZAYA: I know.

SALIM: My flight isn't leaving until so late tonight tho humare paas pura din hai together, and it's going to be really special, hai na? You're coming to my mosque, we're going to shop for my mom's gift, we'll come back here and watch one of my feminist Bollywood movies—and no, *Aaja Nachle* does not count—we can have a little dance party even though you hate dancing and then we'll open our fasts. I love this day.

ZAYA: Sounds like everything I want to do.

SALIM: Hey, we agreed to this weeks ago.

ZAYA: I know, I know. I'm happy to do whatever you want today. Seriously.

SALIM: Acha tho phir let's—

ZAYA: Except for sleeping right now. Let's just keep talking! Please!

A little silence.

You know, this will be the longest we've ever been apart . . . I can't stop thinking about it, sorry. Two months without you seems . . .

SALIM: Zaya, tumko patha hai ke this trip is something my mom and I have been thinking about for years.

ZAYA: Yeah yeah, for sure. I just think, like, going to bed without you for two months will be hard.

SALIM: Oh, but right now you don't want to.

ZAYA: Salim.

SALIM: Pyaare, meh sirf keh rahi hoon ke today's the last Friday before Eid, so we have to be extra good.

SALIM unhooks their bra playfully.

Allah's watching us right now. I hope yeh aapko patha hai.

ZAYA: So?

SALIM: So if we sleep now we can kill a few hours and that'll make fasting easier, hai na?

ZAYA: You think I'm gonna break my fast.

SALIM: Zaya . . .

ZAYA: Oh my god, Salim, I'm not going to break my fast.

SALIM: You said this last Ramzaan . . .

ZAYA: Okay, but how many times are we gonna talk about that? I was hungover / that day and I accidentally ate the—

SALIM: Zaya, it's been four years, and every year you try to keep one fast for me, aur meh yeh appreciate karti hoon, I do, I appreciate you trying, but it would mean a lot to me if you could actually keep one. Purey din ke liye.

ZAYA: I will. Today. I will. Today is going to be really special. I won't break my fast, I promise.

Beat.

You don't believe me.

SALIM: You love me?

ZAYA: Oh my god you don't believe me.

SALIM: I believe you, pyaare.

ZAYA: I'm gonna be so good today.

ZAYA holds SALIM.

SALIM: Okay. So, bedtime.

SALIM tries to get up; ZAYA kisses them.

Zaya, it's almost eight-thirty. A.M.

ZAYA nods and kisses SALIM again.

Our day itna lamba ho ga if we don't sleep . . .

ZAYA nods and kisses SALIM again.

We can't piss off Allah today . . .

ZAYA: I don't wanna talk anymore. Can I blow you now?

SALIM sighs.

SALIM: Yes.

> *They laugh. ZAYA goes down on SALIM, who rests their arms on his shoulders. MAULANA appears, standing over them. ZAYA continues blowing SALIM but stops when MAULANA clears his throat.*

Kya hua?

ZAYA looks at MAULANA in slight disbelief, then back at SALIM.

Kya dekh / rahey ho?

ZAYA: Nothing, sorry.

SALIM: If you don't want to do this—

ZAYA: No, no, I wanna blow you. I'm sorry.

> *ZAYA manages to ignore MAULANA—who stands in his periphery—as he kisses SALIM. ZAYA goes back down on SALIM. MAULANA speaks to ZAYA.*

MAULANA: Beta, take it out your mouth.

ZAYA stops blowing SALIM again.

ZAYA: Okay, Salim, sorry, but I can't really concentrate when your bangles are digging into my shoulders.

SALIM: Oh . . . Concentrate? I'm fine if you autopilot.

ZAYA: Can you take them off?

SALIM: Kyun? I'll just be careful.

ZAYA: No. Please.

SALIM: Okay meh tumko touch / nahi karungi.

SALIM takes their arms off ZAYA.

ZAYA: I want you to touch me.

SALIM: Zaya, maybe we should stop.

ZAYA: I really want this, Salim.

SALIM: It just—it takes so long to take them off.

ZAYA: Let me help you.

ZAYA tries to take off SALIM's bangles quickly while looking over to see if MAULANA is still there.

SALIM: Ow, Zaya, okay, aise mat karo.

ZAYA: Sorry.

SALIM: Ow, Zaya, stop!

ZAYA tries to focus on taking off the bangles but ends up accidentally breaking one, which cuts SALIM's hand and his own thumb. SALIM gets up.

SALIM & ZAYA: Fuck!

ZAYA: Salim, I'm sorry.

SALIM: My hand's bleeding.

SALIM leaves. ZAYA puts his thumb in his mouth.

MAULANA: Beta, please take it out your mouth.

Beat.

Arey, I say take it out your mouth, but you keep sucking, sucking, sucking, sucking, sucking—arey!

MAULANA walks over to ZAYA and pulls him around, gently taking his thumb out of his mouth.

You not listen me why, huh? Aur, how you wear no pant to Islamiyat class? You must respect this masjid—this my home too, okay?

ZAYA: Wait . . . Maulana saab?

MAULANA: Yes! Why you look me like this? How you forget where we are? This ispecial room is Islamiyat class where we learn how to be good musilmaan! I help you. First thing: good musilmaan wear pant.

MAULANA picks up ZAYA's pants and gives them to him. ZAYA doesn't take them right away. MAULANA waits. ZAYA puts them on.

Second thing: don't keep sucking sucking sucking on thumb! Especially in this ispecial time. It is Ramzaan, you have to be extra good. Dekho beta, there is time aur place for taking off pant aur sucking thumb. Okay? Okay?

ZAYA: Uh . . .

MAULANA: You have to alway try to be so good like you are pure shiny gold istar. You gonna try to be like that?

Beat.

Answer me.

ZAYA: Oh. Uh. Yeah?

A phone starts to ring.

MAULANA: Good! Istay here. I am come back to see how good you be in class.

ZAYA: Wait, what???

MAULANA leaves and SALIM enters with ZAYA's cellphone.

SALIM: Zaya? Your phone.

ZAYA: Where'd you go?

SALIM: Washroom. My hand was bleeding.

ZAYA: Oh. Right, sorry about your bangles.

SALIM: Can you just take this? It's your sister.

SALIM gives the phone to ZAYA, and he answers it.

ZAYA: Hello? Hi, Laila.

Beat.

What? When?

Beat.

Okay, and why can't you—yeah, fine, okay, I'll get there as soon as I can.

ZAYA hangs up, then looks back to make sure MAULANA is gone.

SALIM: What's wrong? Zaya? You are still high, aren't you? Tumko paani chahiye ya—

ZAYA: I'm fine.

SALIM: Tho Laila ne kya kaha?

ZAYA: Uh. We have to go to the hospital. Credit Valley.

SALIM: Kyun? Kya hua?

ZAYA: My, uh, my ma just fell.

SALIM: Oh god. I'm sorry, Zaya. Is she okay?

ZAYA: I think. so She tripped on something. Laila said she's just a little shaken up but she's mobile, so . . .

SALIM: Okay. Okay, tho meh tumko drop off kar sakti hoon aur phir—

ZAYA: Can you stay with me? Please.

SALIM: In the hospital? With your mom?

ZAYA: Well yeah, kind of. I mean—in the lobby.

SALIM: In the lobby?

ZAYA: I just have to make sure she's all right. I'll only be half an hour.

SALIM: No you won't.

ZAYA: Okay, forty-five minutes max. I'm gonna see her again on Eid, so I promise I won't be long.

SALIM: Meh drop off kar sakti hoon aur wapas aaney mein you can take the 21B / because it stops right outside—

ZAYA: Salim, please, I just want you there.

SALIM: I don't want to wait in a hospital lobby in Mississauga for forty-five minutes.

ZAYA: Well I really don't want to be apart from you today.

SALIM: Tho phir let me see your mom.

ZAYA: Come on. Salim, you know I can't do that.

SALIM: You can't?

ZAYA: She's just—she probably will be in a terrible mood today.

Beat.

And I wouldn't want you to change anything about yourself for her, right. So let me—give me some time and I'll talk to her and, and when you get back from your trip we can—maybe try . . .

SALIM: Teekh hai it's fine. I just—I need to be back here in Toronto by eleven, okay? I still need to get some sleep and then be ready for prayer by one. Aur hum late nahi ho saktey hain kyun ke the mosque is going to throw me a little farewell send-off party after prayer / and it just doesn't look good if—

ZAYA: Fine, fine. Then let's go now.

SALIM: Teekh hai. I'll pray two rakaat for your mom then we'll go.

ZAYA: What??

SALIM: Kya? Just two rakaat.

ZAYA: Seriously?

SALIM: Kya matlab? I'm praying for your mom's health.

ZAYA: It won't make a difference.

SALIM: Sorry?

ZAYA: Nothing.

SALIM: Just two rakaat, Zaya. This is important. And I'd like you to join me.

SALIM leaves. ZAYA starts to follow. MAULANA enters with a single ja-namaz.

MAULANA: Beta, I like to tell you something. Please, have a sit. Yes yes, no worry, no worry, you can sit in my spot. Please.

MAULANA gestures to a specific spot on the ground. ZAYA doesn't sit.

Acha teekh hai, you don't have to. I sit, I like to sit.

MAULANA sets his ja-namaz down and sits on it, facing ZAYA.

You know this, it is not very lonely down here when I sit by myself. You want to know why? We are never alone. Allah'tala alway with us. Yes, people come aur go, come aur go, come aur go in our life, but one thing remain forever is Allah'tala.

ZAYA: I don't think so.

MAULANA: You don't think so? You don't feel his presence right now?

ZAYA: No.

MAULANA: Tho why don't you try praying with me? Hm? Then I am sure—

ZAYA: No. I'm not going to do that.

MAULANA: Kyun nahi?

ZAYA: Well I—I think it's a trap.

MAULANA: Oh no no no, beta! Prayer is the key to freedom. When you ispeak with love, when you ispeak from the truth of your heart to Allah'tala during prayer, you will be free. If you ever feel lost, beta, he will guide you. I promise. I promise ke you will feel better one day.

ZAYA: Feel better about what?

MAULANA: I am sorry for your family loss. I am sorry ke your daddy leave you.

ZAYA: My dad?

MAULANA: It is not fair how he leave just like that, aur meh aapse kehna chatha hoon ke it is not your fault. It is not your fault. Aur if you can believe, the most good thing come from this is knowing ke you are not alone, okay? You are never alone.

A little silence.

Please sit with me, beta.

After a moment, ZAYA sits down.

Verily, with every hardship, there is relief. Verily, with every hardship, there is relief. Okay? You will find relief. I know you will. I believe in you.

MAULANA reaches out and touches ZAYA's shoulder.

You are very isensitive boy. It is good. I like to ispend more time with you. More Islamiyat class. You want?

MUBEEN enters holding up his cricket bat covered in gold stars along the sides.

MUBEEN: Abba abba can I—

MAULANA removes his hand from ZAYA and gets up. MUBEEN sees this.

MAULANA: Ah, Mubeen!

ZAYA: Mubeen?

MUBEEN: Oh. I just wanna show Zaya the cricket bat you got me.

MAULANA: Beta, there is time aur place for cricket bat. Please, give me.

MUBEEN: Abba, pleeeease . . . Zaya, quick, look there's / gold stars—

MAULANA: Mubeen.

MUBEEN hesitates, then hands over the cricket bat.

Good. Now you are here, why don't you share with Zaya what I teach you yesterday, hmm?

MUBEEN: Oh, uhhh . . .

MAULANA: English translation of surah falaq! Come on, my son, you know this. Chalo, istart to teach him aur I bring down more ja-namaz aur phir together we all pray. Okay, Zaya?

ZAYA nods.

Good. You listen good today. Thank you, Zaya.

MAULANA leaves with the cricket bat.

MUBEEN: What's going on? Why you look so sad? Clearly you doing so good in Islamiyat now. You should be happy; you should be dancing around!

Beat.

God you're so boring when you act all shy and quiet! Why you looking at me like that?

ZAYA: Like what?

MUBEEN: Like how you looking at me right now.

ZAYA: I'm—not . . .

MUBEEN: What do you want, huh? What do you want?

ZAYA: Nothing.

MUBEEN: God, I told you this before. You just gotta ask for what you want.

Beat. MUBEEN kisses ZAYA.

ZAYA: Hey, whoa!

MUBEEN: What?

MUBEEN kisses ZAYA again. ZAYA moves away and unknowingly steps onto the edge of the ja-namaz. He looks over to see if MAULANA is around.

ZAYA: I don't think we should do that.

MUBEEN: I was just—but we always—fine. Whatever. I don't wanna do this no more anyways. In fact, I never wanna do it in the first place. You always make me. What? Don't act all shocked. You always touching me and tricking me. It's all your fault. So no more. Also, I love Sadiya, by the way. I forgot to tell you. Sorry.

ZAYA: What??

MUBEEN: Don't act like you care. You wanna change now, right? You tryna be so good now, right? Why? My abba don't actually care about you.

MUBEEN sees that ZAYA is standing on the ja-namaz.

OH MY GOD, and don't stand on that unless you gonna pray. But you don't even know how!

MUBEEN takes the ja-namaz.

God, you can't do anything right. You never gonna be good. But go ahead. Try. Change.

MUBEEN leaves and SALIM enters.

SALIM: Where did you go?

ZAYA: When?

SALIM: Just right now. Nurse hum se baat kar rahi thi. You weren't listening.

ZAYA: Oh shit, sorry, can you tell me what the nurse said?

SALIM: So you didn't—your mom's resting now. The arthritis in her knees swelled up and they're just waiting on scans to know if she fractured her wrist or not. Most likely it's sprained.

ZAYA: Okay. Wow. Sorry. I've just been—you know, it's weird, I've been thinking about—well just earlier this morning I started thinking about this—uh, I'm just thinking about other things.

SALIM: Like what?

ZAYA: Just—I'm remembering this maulana I used to have as a kid—and I used to go to his masjid a lot, like my mom would drop me off for the day on weekends and I think every day after school I'd also . . . This was like twenty years ago, so, yeah.

SALIM: Okay. Mujhe aur batha saktey ho?

ZAYA: Uhhh, the maulana had a son. He was a couple years older than me. And there would be these gatherings at, at the masjid, like . . . It's so funny, I don't even know why I'm thinking about it. I can't even really remember—you know, actually, I don't wanna talk about it.

SALIM: Zaya, agar yehi waja hai for why you've been so quiet since we left our place—I think we should talk about it.

ZAYA: It's fine, seriously. I was just distracted.

SALIM: Pyaare, you know you can talk to me. Meh hoon tumhare saath.

ZAYA: Thank you, Salim, I know. I actually just don't wanna think about it right now. Thanks.

Beat.

What's the time?

SALIM: Almost ten.

ZAYA: Wow, seriously??

SALIM: Kya?

ZAYA: Ma's been here by herself for over an hour. Oh shit!

SALIM: Ab kya hua, Zaya?

ZAYA: Laila told me to bring a change of clothes for Ma and I . . . shit!

SALIM: Okay, Zaya, it's okay, it's okay. You want me to get them?

ZAYA: No, no, I can.

SALIM: Likhen phir mujhe tumko drive karna hai to your mom's place and then drive you back here.

ZAYA: I can walk.

SALIM: It's a twenty-minute walk and a five-minute drive. We're in Mississauga, remember? Meh jaathi hoon.

ZAYA: You sure?

SALIM: Yes, pyaare. Now what does she want? Shalwar kameez?

ZAYA: No, she um, she really likes her blouses from Fairweather, so maybe one of those and some pants.

SALIM: Fairweather. Got it.

ZAYA: Salim. Don't laugh.

SALIM: Oh, kabhie nahi.

Beat.

Okay so, should I break in through the window or do you wanna give me the house key . . .

ZAYA: Oh, right. Here. It's this one.

ZAYA gives his keys to SALIM.

Just make sure you please call me when you get back and I can take the clothes from you, okay?

SALIM: Teekh hai.

ZAYA: Thank you.

ZAYA kisses SALIM.

SALIM: Of course. I'll be back soon. Allah'hafiz.

SALIM starts to leave.

ZAYA: And . . . Thank you for praying for her, Salim.

SALIM: Of course.

SALIM leaves. ZAYA turns around and sees MA. She is in a hospital gown, sleeping. He walks very carefully and positions himself next to her. He gently strokes her hair. She slowly starts to wake up.

ZAYA: Oh, hey, pretty woman. Hey . . .

MA fully opens her eyes and slaps ZAYA's hand away.

MA: Hey hey, ka bacha, salaam karne bul gaye?

ZAYA: Oh my god, Ma, I was just saying hi.

MA: Tho phir salaam karo.

ZAYA: Assalaam'olaikum.

MA: Good. Walekum'assalaam.

MA inspects ZAYA.

Arey, yeh patiwi pant kyun pein rahey ho?

MA touches the rips in ZAYA's jeans.

ZAYA: It's fashion, Ma. I love your outfit.

MA: Shukriya. You look tired.

ZAYA: Oh, thank you.

MA: You are sleeping?

ZAYA: Yes. Kind of. Look, I know you aren't sleeping. You fell this morning way before you usually wake up. Are you okay? How's your wrist?

MA: Teekh hai.

ZAYA: How did it happen? How did you fall?

MA: Mera shawl floor pey tha.

ZAYA: Why was your shawl on the floor?

MA: Mujhe kaise patha?

ZAYA: Seriously?

MA: Kya seriously? I don't see it aur meh girgayi. Next time I open my eye meh yahan pey hoon. Since eight-thirty A.M.!!!

ZAYA: Sorry . . . I got delayed getting here.

MA: Kaise aayo?

ZAYA: My friend drove me.

MA: Kaun?

ZAYA: Salim. The teacher? Remember? The one who would ask for your biryani recipe / every time—

MA: Oh. Haan, haan.

ZAYA: Yeah, they're just—Salim's just—we've got a lot of things to do today . . . So I actually can't stay too long. I'm sorry.

MA: Kyun?

ZAYA: Well I need a ride back home.

MA: Laila dey sakti hai.

ZAYA: No, she can't. I'm pretty sure she said she can't get here for a few hours.

MA: Tho phir wait karo. Mere saath.

ZAYA: I can't. I told you I've got things to do today.

MA: Work hai?

ZAYA: No, but I—

MA: Tho phir kya?

ZAYA: Well Salim's leaving for a big trip tonight and—actually, Salim's gonna do Umrah. With their mom.

MA: Hm.

ZAYA: You know, Mecca. The pilgrimage thing?

MA: Tum mujhe Umrah explain karo gey?

ZAYA: No, sorry. Uh, so Salim needs to finish packing and buy a gift for their mom and I wanna help with that, so . . .

MA: Uske paas koi aur friends nahi hai jo—

ZAYA: Ma, I want to help.

MA: Tho phir yahan kyun aayo?

ZAYA: I want to see you. I just can't stay too long.

MA: Faida kya hai?

ZAYA: Ma, come on, I'll see you in two days for Eid.

MA: Nahi nahi, tum jao. Agar tum jaana chathey hai tho jao, aur meh yahan akheli mar jaaongi. Teekh hai?

ZAYA: Don't say that. You're not gonna die, Ma.

MA: Tumko kaise patha?

ZAYA: The nurse said you're fine.

MA: Nurse don't know ke I have son who don't care for me. Meh aisi mar jaaongi, I guarantee you!

ZAYA: Ma, I do care about you—I do.

MA: Good. Tho phir aaj mere saath gahar aao. Bas. Yeh done deal hai.

ZAYA: Ma—

MA: No more Ma Ma Ma! No, no!

ZAYA can't say anything. He checks his phone for a text from SALIM. *Nothing. He puts it away.*

ZAYA: Hey, so um, just this morning I started thinking about that masjid we used to go to, like twenty years ago. You remember it?

MA: Kaun sa masjid?

ZAYA: It was in the basement of a house. You sent Laila and me there every day after school for a couple of months or something.

MA: Oh, haan haan.

ZAYA: Do you—remember anything about it? Like, do you remember walking down the stairs and wasn't the smaller prayer room on the—

MA: Beta, why you are asking me? Mujhe nahi patha . . .

ZAYA: But do you remember anything about it? Do you remember when the masjid closed down? The day after Eid that year?

MA: Twenty year ago is so long time, kaise yeh umeed rakh saktey ho ke mujhe / yeh sab yaad ho ga?

ZAYA: You remember the maulana saab at least, right?

Beat. MA nods.

Okay, and his son Mubeen? Or, Farah auntie? Do you still keep in touch with any of the aunties?

MA: Haan, hum . . . baat kartey hain.

ZAYA: What about Naima auntie? She was always so loud, right? And remember her daughter Sadiya? Laila's old friend?

MA: Oh haan, Sadiya, very sweet girl. Acha ab bathao, tumhari biwi kahan hai?

ZAYA: What??

MA: Kab shaadi karo gey?

ZAYA: I'm not talking about this.

ZAYA checks his phone again.

MA: Kyun nahi?

ZAYA: I told you before, I'm not ready.

MA: Kab ready ho gey? You are twenty-eight . . .

ZAYA: So what?

MA: Tho jab mein yahan se nik lungi, meh seedhi Pakistan jaongi aur tumhari pretty woman ko ley kar aaongi here. Bas.

ZAYA: No, thank you.

MA: No thank you ka bacha, tum kaun si type ki ladki pasand karte ho? Bathao na. Bathao na beta!!!

ZAYA: Okay! Okay okay.

Beat.

I like naughty girls, I guess.

MA: Teekh hai. I find naughty girl for you. Mallika Sherawat jaisi.

ZAYA: Great. I like Mallika.

MA: Yeh joke nahi hai.

ZAYA: I'm not joking either.

Beat.

And when are you gonna get married?

MA: Zaya.

ZAYA: What?

MA: Aise mat joke karna mere saath.

ZAYA: No, I'm actually serious, Ma. I think you're strong, and beautiful, and smart, and funny. And young.

MA: Haan haan, meh yeh sab kuch hoon, aur bahot busy too.

ZAYA: I can make your profile on shaadi.com.

MA: Arey chup!

ZAYA: Laila can take your photo when you get home.

MA: Yeh nahi ho sakta hai. Meh busy hoon.

ZAYA: Oh yeah? Doing what?

MA: Meri pehli appointment afternoo—

MA stops herself.

ZAYA: Appointment? For what? Wait. For like cutting hair? Ma, we've talked about this. Laila and I can pay for stuff. You don't have to be working.

MA: Oh haan haan, bilkul bilkul. Eid two days mein hai, busy busy time of year for me, aur I don't work? / Good idea, beta!

ZAYA: Oh my god, just retire already!!

MA: Mera kam important hai. All my client depend me. Meh koi retail shetail mein kam nahi karti hoon.

ZAYA: Okay, just so we're clear, I'm a store manager.

MA: You fold clothes.

ZAYA: Ma!

MA: Ma, Ma, ka bacha, such nahi hai?

ZAYA: We're not talking about me. This is about you and it's serious and I just don't think you understand—

SALIM enters—makeup and jewellery removed, wearing something a little less feminine—with MA's change of clothes in a Thiara Supermarket plastic bag.

Salim?

SALIM: Assalaam'olaikum, Auntie.

ZAYA: What are you doing here?

SALIM: *(to MA)* Yeh aapke liye. Change of clothes.

ZAYA: Salim, you said you were going to—

SALIM: Aap kaisi hain? It's been so long.

(to ZAYA) Is she doing okay?

ZAYA: Ma, I'll be right back. We're just gonna be in—

SALIM: Auntie, meh ne aapke liye yeh shirt-pant ley kar aa—um, is that okay? Do you like these?

ZAYA: Okay, can we talk outside?

SALIM: Zaya, you said this is what she wanted.

ZAYA: It is!

Beat.

Ma, look, Salim brought your change of clothes. Shirt and pants.

ZAYA takes the bag from SALIM and offers it to MA.

Here. Take them. Ma?

MA: I want shalwar kameez.

ZAYA: What?

MA: Meh yeh shirt pant nahi peinthi hoon.

SALIM: Acha teekh hai, Auntie.

ZAYA: No, Salim, it's fine. She'll wear these.

SALIM: Auntie, do you want me to get your shalwar kameez right now?

SALIM crouches next to MA and rests their hand over hers. She sees their painted nails. So does ZAYA. SALIM registers their own painted nails. MA takes her hand away and turns from SALIM.

ZAYA: Salim . . .

SALIM, very self-conscious now, tries to carry on.

SALIM: Auntie, meh idhar hoon.

ZAYA: Salim. I think she's tired. Can you please wait for me outside?

SALIM: I don't want to wait outside. I'm trying to talk to your mom right now.

ZAYA: Well she doesn't feel like talking.

SALIM: Can you let her speak for herself?

ZAYA: Salim, please just stop.

SALIM: Zaya, yeh mere liye important / hai ke meh—

ZAYA: Salim, I said enough!

A little silence. SALIM takes a step back. They look at MA, then back at ZAYA and then they leave. ZAYA looks at MA, who doesn't look at him. He can't say anything. He follows SALIM out into the hallway.

Wait. Salim, wait. Please.

SALIM stops.

You said you would call me when you got back.

SALIM: I wanted to see your mom.

ZAYA: But that's not what—you should've asked me / first if that—

SALIM: Kyun mujhe permission chahiye, Zaya?

ZAYA: Because you know how she is.

SALIM: Kaisi hain? Mujhe bathao.

ZAYA: Ma saw your painted nails. And that makes her uncomfortable, so she . . . Salim, look, it was different before—right, so, we can't just surprise her with things like that.

SALIM: I wasn't trying to surprise her.

ZAYA: Then what?

SALIM: I forgot about my nails. Honestly. Meh samjhi thi ke taking my makeup off and changing my clothes would be enough.

ZAYA: Well it wasn't.

SALIM: Aur ab mujhe yeh patha hai, okay?

ZAYA: I—I know this is hard for you. So maybe after your trip we could . . .

SALIM: You used to really want us to have a relationship. You used to love when I'd come over for dinner at her place. You thought it was funny when she and I would talk about *Humsafar*.

ZAYA: That was like three years ago, Salim. She needs time to adjust to how you've changed.

SALIM: You've changed too.

ZAYA: I know that.

SALIM: Tho yeh humare liye kya matlab hai?

ZAYA: I think it just means we leave Ma alone right now and we don't fight, and we just go back to the really exciting day you've planned for us.

ZAYA, in his sarcasm, tries to make SALIM smile as he holds them.

Doesn't that sound so good . . .

SALIM: I wanted to properly say bye to her.

ZAYA: Can we please stop talking about my mom? Today is supposed to be about us.

SALIM: Meh humare baare mein baat kar rahi hoon.

ZAYA: You know, do you ever find it strange how we've probably spent a million hours talking about my relationship to Ma when in the years I've known you I've never met yours, or even known when she's in town?

SALIM: Zaya, yeh kyun—that's so unrelated . . .

ZAYA: How?

SALIM: Woh yahan pey nahi reh thi hai, her schedule is unpredictable and / she moves around a lot so you—

ZAYA: So? I'd still love to meet her. I think that could be a really important step for us. Don't you? Don't you think?

SALIM: It's different because you've never had a relationship with my mom.

ZAYA: But why is that? Why do you keep us apart?

SALIM: Keep you apart? Really?

ZAYA: Do you think I might not meet her standards?

SALIM: It's not like that.

ZAYA: She might think I'm too poor?

SALIM: Zaya, aise baatein mat karo.

ZAYA: Or maybe you just think I'm not good enough.

SALIM: What? Why would I think that? Why would I think that about you?

A little silence.

You know, jab meh keh sakti hoon, I tell you I love you. And I mean it. I need you to start believing me, or . . . Aur kya kar sakti hoon meh?

MUBEEN enters with a shiny gift box.

MUBEEN: Zaya?

ZAYA: Mubeen? Oh my god.

ZAYA goes to MUBEEN. They look at each other. ZAYA goes to hug MUBEEN but then stops. Beat. Then they hug each other.

What . . . What are you doing here?

MUBEEN: I-I came to just drop off some sweets for your amma.

ZAYA: What?

MUBEEN: I thought maybe it'd cheer her up or something. It's barfi.

SALIM: She's diabetic.

ZAYA: Salim. Oh! Uh. Salim. Uhhh, this is Mubeen.

MUBEEN: Hi.

MUBEEN and SALIM shake hands. MUBEEN looks at SALIM's nails.

SALIM: Hello.

ZAYA: Salim, Mubeen and I are old childhood friends . . .

SALIM: Oh. Wow.

MUBEEN: Yeah but we haven't seen each / other in—

ZAYA: Yeah, it's been a while. Twenty years or something.

MUBEEN: Well, more like ten years.

ZAYA: Ten years? Oh yeah yeah yeah. Right, right.

MUBEEN: Um, yeah so. How do / you two know—

ZAYA: Wait, so how'd you know my mom was here? In the hospital?

MUBEEN: She called my abba this morning.

ZAYA: What? Why?

MUBEEN: She asked him to pray for her. For her health. He's running juma prayer today so all the people who show up to that will pray for her too.

ZAYA: Oh, okay . . . He's still . . .

MUBEEN: Oh yeah, I mean you can never stop being a maulana, am I right?

SALIM: Uh huh. So, where's the prayer held?

MUBEEN: In Kitchener. In our home.

(to ZAYA) Yeah, we've been in Kitchener since we left Mississauga so . . . Anyways, we do juma prayer every week. Oh, I meant Friday prayer. We do—

SALIM: I know what juma means. Meh Urdu bhi bol sakti hoon.

MUBEEN: Oh. Okay.

SALIM: We're going to a different mosque for juma today, but we should go one time, hai na, Zaya?

ZAYA: Well I don't know if Kitchener—

MUBEEN: Well, you have to be Muslim.

ZAYA: / Mubeen.

SALIM: Oh, I am.

MUBEEN: Oh. Do you practise?

ZAYA: / Mubeen.

SALIM: Yes, I do.

MUBEEN: Well, our home's pretty small, so we can't fit a lot of people, and we've already / got families who show up every week so—

ZAYA: Mubeen, it's okay, it's okay, we understand.

MUBEEN: Okay.

Beat.

So, how do you two know each other?

SALIM looks at ZAYA, waiting for his response.

ZAYA: We met in our undergrad.

(to SALIM) Fourth year, right?

SALIM: To be more specific, Mubeen, we met at a Muslim Students Association meeting, actually. I caught Zaya checking out one of our posters and invited him to join us. Then we went for drinks, we danced—well, I danced—and I think we hooked up / that night.

ZAYA: Salim!

MUBEEN: Oh cool. So you're both . . .

SALIM: Muslim, yes.

MUBEEN: Oh no, I meant, you're . . .

ZAYA: We're together! Yes, we're, we're . . . partners.

MUBEEN: Oh, cool. That's . . . cool.

SALIM: Cool.

(to ZAYA) Partner.

ZAYA: So uh, Mubeen, Ma's room is actually just down the hall.

MUBEEN: Oh yeah, I know. I got the room number, so . . .

ZAYA: I can—go with you, if you want . . .

MUBEEN: I mean, I don't wanna interrupt if you two need to talk or uhh—never mind. Sure, yeah, let's go.

ZAYA: Okay, just a second.

(to SALIM) I'll be out of there in ten minutes. If you can please just wait a little longer. And then we'll leave. I promise. I just have to . . .

SALIM sighs.

SALIM: Teekh hai. Ten minutes.

ZAYA: Yes. Okay.

(to MUBEEN) All right. Ready to go?

MUBEEN: Yeah. Uh, good to meet you, Salim.

SALIM: Such a pleasure to meet you, Mubeen. I'm sorry I hadn't heard anything about you before.

MUBEEN: Oh uh, it's okay. Um, take care.

SALIM: Allah'hafiz, Mubeen.

SALIM leaves. ZAYA and MUBEEN start to walk towards MA's room.

ZAYA: Um, you—you just never really came up, honestly. Sorry if—

MUBEEN: Don't worry about it. Hey, can I ask you something?

ZAYA: Sure.

Beat.

MUBEEN: Is he hitting you?

ZAYA: Sorry?

MUBEEN: Oh my god, don't act stupid. Tell me the truth. You not supposda lie this month anyways. It's Ramzaan.

ZAYA: Oh shit . . .

MUBEEN: Stop avoiding the question. Is my abba hitting you?

ZAYA: I, I . . .

MUBEEN: TELL ME.

Beat.

Zaya, come on, please. I needa know what's going on. He, he—he took away all my Islamiyat classes and gave them to you, you know that? I didn't even do anything really that wrong and now I gotta finish reading the Qur'an all by myself? You know how unfair that is?! And and, he said he was gonna give me back my cricket bat but it's been over a week now . . . So, like, why is he treating me like this??

ZAYA: I don't know.

MUBEEN: Yeah you do, don't lie! Something's going on cuz you been acting different to me too lately, like I don't even exist, and and, you know I can hear the music? Sometimes I hear music coming outta the basement when you in class. Sadiya hear it too, you know, so so so—what's going on? Is, is my abba using music to, like, cover the sounds? So like like, we can't hear him hitting you over the music? Is that it? Is that what the music is for?

ZAYA: I'm . . . not sure.

MUBEEN: You not sure??

ZAYA: I can't remember.

MUBEEN: You can't remember?? You just had class yesterday! You gotta stop lying, it's so bad for you. Just tell me. Did he hit you or not?

A silence. MUBEEN gets closer.

You can tell me. Why won't you tell me? Is it really bad? Is he . . . beating you up? Is he beating you up? Oh my god, if he is, you gotta tell me, Zaya. You gotta tell me right now. Oh god no, is he, is he hitting you with my cricket bat? Oh god no, not my cricket bat—it's MY cricket bat! This is, this is real bad. Zaya, if he's doing something real bad to you, you gotta make sure you don't tell no one else, okay? Just tell me. I'll, I'll do something to fix it, I promise. Just tell me. Or, you know what, if you're feeling so sad, you don't even gotta say it. Just show me. Show me your bruises.

MUBEEN tries to lift up ZAYA's shirt. ZAYA pushes MUBEEN's arm away and takes a step back.

ZAYA: No! He—I don't think he . . .

MUBEEN: Then what?? WHAT'S GOING ON? Oh my god, Zaya, are you—are you doing something to him?

MA suddenly appears in her hospital bed. ZAYA moves towards her.

MA: Zaya, kahan thay?

ZAYA: Ma, Mubeen's here.

MA: Mubeen?

MUBEEN appears to MA.

MUBEEN: Assalaam'olaikum, Auntie.

MA: Ah! Walekum'assalaam, beta.

MUBEEN: Uh. Yeh aapke liye.

MUBEEN gives MA the shiny gift box.

MA: Oh mere liye? Barfi, hai na? My favourite! Shukriya.

MUBEEN: Koi baat nahi, Auntie.

MA: Acha beta bathao mujhe, kaise ho?

MUBEEN: Teekh takh, Auntie, teekh takh. Aap kaisi hain?

MA: Meh tho teekh hi hoon . . . Thoda sa pain hai.

MUBEEN: I'm sorry you fell, Auntie.

MA: Haan, chalo, yeh sab chodho. Tum bahot achey lag rahey ho, Mubeen. Very strong aur healthy. Mash'allah.

MUBEEN: Shukriya, Auntie.

MA: Aur . . . maulana saab kaise hain?

MUBEEN: Woh bhi teekh hai, Auntie. Allah ka shukhar.

MA: Good. Aur how is Kitchery?

MUBEEN: Kitchery?

ZAYA: Kitchener, Ma.

MA: Haan haan jo bhi hai.

MUBEEN: Oh yeah, Kitchener's great, Auntie. Aapko patha hai, today everyone at our masjid aapke health ke liye pray kar rahey hain.

MA: Oh. Thank you. Aur meh already bahot better feel kar rahi hoon. Allah ka shukhar.

MUBEEN: Allah ka shukhar.

Beat.

Acha, Auntie, meh ja tha hoon. I have to go to work now, so . . .

ZAYA: Uh hey, thanks for stopping by. Can I get you something on your way out? Coffee or anything?

MA: Zaya, he is fasting today.

(to MUBEEN) Hai na, beta?

MUBEEN: Yeah, sorry.

ZAYA: Oh. Right. Sorry.

MUBEEN: Acha, Auntie, please, kayal rakhna aur insh'allah I'll see you and Laila next Friday. / Sorry you can't—

ZAYA: Wait, what? Next / Friday? What's going on—

MA: *(to MUBEEN)* Okay, / allah'hafiz mera, beta.

MUBEEN: My nikah's next Friday. It's okay, I know you can't make it. Won't be a wild party or anything. No dancing. No music even, actually.

ZAYA: Oh. I didn't see the invite.

MUBEEN: Oh, that's strange. Well, there's a little note on the gift box with all the wedding info and my cell, so if you can make it, you could just give me a call and RSVP. You don't have to though. Just, here.

MUBEEN takes the note from the gift box and gives it to ZAYA.

Uh. Mubeen Shaikh weds Sadiya Ahmed. It's uh nice, isn't it?

ZAYA: Oh. Yeah.

MUBEEN: Would've been nice to have you there, but maybe I'll see you around or, um . . . Uh, never mind. Good to see you after so long.

Okay. Allah'hafiz, Auntie.

MA: Allah'hafiz, beta.

MUBEEN leaves.

ZAYA: What was that?

MA: Kya?

ZAYA: You're being weird.

MA: Meh weird nahi hoon. Tum weird ho.

ZAYA: No, like you're being fake, like you weren't happy to see Mubeen or something.

MA: Kya keh rahey ho? Meh khush thi. You want cartwheel?

ZAYA: No, I just thought you haven't seen him in like twenty years, so—okay, wait, I don't understand. You're hiding things from me.

MA: Kya?

ZAYA: How long have you known about Mubeen's wedding?

MA: Arey, chodho, Zaya. Yeh tho big deal nahi hai.

ZAYA: How long have you been talking to Mubeen's dad?

MA: Kya?

ZAYA: How long have you been talking to him?

MA: Kya problem hai, Zaya? Meh sirf Farah se baat karti hoon once ya twice per year, teekh hai?

ZAYA: Mubeen said you called his dad this morning.

MA: Meh Farah ko call kar rahi thi aur he pick up.

ZAYA: Seriously? Ma, are you lying to me?

MA: Kya baat kar rahey ho! Meh kabhie jhoot bolthi hoon?

ZAYA: Ma, if you've been talking to him, I just wanna know how long this has been going on for.

MA: Kyun? Kya zaroorat hai investigation / ki?

ZAYA: Answer me, please!

MA: Since he move to Kitchery—Kitchener—jo bhi hai. Ab jawab mil gaya? Khush ho?

ZAYA: Why? Why have you been talking to him / for all these years?

MA: Yeh kaisa sawal hai! Woh maulana saab hai.

ZAYA: So what?

MA: Tho I respect him.

ZAYA: You respect him??

MA: Woh acha aadmi hai.

ZAYA: No, Ma, he's not a good . . . Did you—did you ever find it weird that he held his private Islamiyat classes in that little room in the basement of the masjid? I mean, I was in those classes a lot, alone with this man, did you—did you ever worry . . .

MA: Worry? Kyun? You love to go to Islamiyat class. Tum itne happy thay when you go.

ZAYA: I was eight.

MA: Tho? Kya kehne chathey ho?

ZAYA: I just wanted . . . I felt—lonely, I needed . . . You were never home.

MA: Zaya, tumko patha tha ke meh three three jobs kar rahi thi.

ZAYA: So?

44

MA: So? Kya matlab? Phir bhi meh tumko school pey drop off karti thi likhen, agar tumhare paas friends nahi thay tho meh kya—

ZAYA: No, that's not what I'm talking about. I'm saying, like, you couldn't tell that maybe something was going on? Like, I was being different?

MA: Kab?

ZAYA: Those months I was in the Islamiyat classes! That's what we're talking about. Don't you remember I started like, like sleeping way more and eating less and I was like quiet all the time? Wasn't I?

MA: Zaya, mujhe yaad nahi hai.

ZAYA: Oh, well maybe you would remember if you actually paid attention to your own kid.

MA: Pay attention?? Yeh tum keh rahey ho? Kuch toh khuda ka kauff karo I give you everything, yeh samajkar ke mera ekhi bacha hai. Aur toh / jaise koi nahi hai sirf you you you!

ZAYA: Ma, that's not what I'm trying to say. / You're not listening to me.

MA: Tum itne zidi thay, you never say ke tum kya feel kar rahey ho likhen har waqt you behave so badly, aur phir bhi I always here for you aur try my best take care of you!

ZAYA: YOU DID NOT TAKE CARE OF ME.

A silence.

MA: Tum yeh kaise keh sakte ho?

ZAYA: You—don't you remember? On Eid that evening, you—you went upstairs, didn't you? I think you left me down there with him and—Ma, listen to me . . . Ma?

SALIM enters with another Thiara Supermarket bag. MA looks away.

SALIM: Zaya?

ZAYA: Salim, this is not a good time.

ZAYA goes to SALIM.

SALIM: Humko jaana hai.

ZAYA: Can you please just give me a minute?

SALIM: No, Zaya, I can't. If we don't leave now, I'm going to be late for my mosque.

ZAYA: Right.

SALIM: Meh ne tumko call kiya a few times but your phone is off.

ZAYA: I have to talk to my ma.

SALIM: Kya ho raha hai?

ZAYA: Nothing, it's fine. It's just not a good time right now.

SALIM: Meh kuch kar sak—

SALIM looks at MA, then chooses to keep speaking.

Meh kuch kar sakti hoon?

ZAYA: You know what, uh, why don't you—why don't you go home without me, and I'll—I can—I'll, I'll meet you there.

SALIM: Zaya.

ZAYA: Salim, please. This is just really . . . I can be home by like three—latest. I promise.

SALIM sighs.

SALIM: Do you need my Presto?

ZAYA: No. Thank you.

SALIM: I picked up your mom's shalwar kameez. Turn your phone on aur mujhe text karo jab tum aarahey ho.

ZAYA: I will.

Beat.

SALIM: You keep pushing me away.

ZAYA: Salim, not now.

SALIM: But I still love you.

Beat. SALIM speaks to MA.

Allah'hafiz, Auntie.

SALIM gives the bag with the shalwar kameez inside to ZAYA and leaves. ZAYA looks at MA. He offers MA the bag. She takes it. He sits down. He can't say anything for a while.

ZAYA: Ma . . . Salim and I are just—

MA: No. Meh Salim ke baare mein nahi baat karna chahathi hoon. I want to talk about you. You say ke I am keeping secrets likhen tumko dekho. You think I am stupid? Meh sab kuch jaanthi hoon, Zaya. Aur, I know everything for very long time. I know how you are. I know what you do. Is liye meh ne sab kuch kiya to help you be good. Sab kuch kiya. Likhen, you always do bad things. Isi waja se masjid close down hua. Aur kya? You do it. Maulana saab tell me. You do this very bad thing to Mubeen twenty year ago aur ab tak tum galat harkatein kar rahey ho.

ZAYA: What bad thing? What have I done?

MA: You know.

Beat.

Likhen, you don't change. Aur, I don't know ke meh aur kya kar sakti hoon to help you. Mujhe nahi patha! Tum bas—jao yahan sey!

ZAYA: Ma, I think maulana saab did something to me.

MA shakes her head and looks away.

I need you to listen to me. Please. Ma?

MA: Zaya! You don't know difference kya hai between real aur fake! Truth aur lie. Right aur wrong. Good aur bad. You like to do bad thing aur meh tumko stop nahi kar sakti hoon. Jo bhi tumko karna hai tum kar thay ho aur meh . . . Meh achi ma nahi hoon, hai na? Meh failure ma hoon, hai na, you want me say this? Mujhe patha hai. Mujhe patha hai for very long time ke I fail you, beta. Meh failure ma hoon.

Beat. ZAYA *gets up and leaves. He goes to the bathroom. He begins to wash his face. Slowly,* MAULANA *appears and watches him.* ZAYA *looks at* MAULANA. *Then he pulls down his pants and faces* MAULANA.

MAULANA: No no no no, pant up. Pant up!

MAULANA takes a step closer to ZAYA.

Ehhhhh you not listen why, huh?? I say pant up! Please, beta.

Slowly, ZAYA *bends over and pulls up his pants.* MAULANA *takes a step towards* ZAYA.

Why you try to hide in this washroom, huh? You can't escape me, beta. Not in this masjid, not in my own home. Why you try escape me? Hmm? No fun? No fun in Islamiyat class?

ZAYA: No. I'm not having fun.

MAULANA: Why not?

ZAYA: I-I don't wanna do this anymore.

MAULANA: You want to dance instead?

ZAYA: What?

MAULANA: Look how your eye get so big when I say dance! You love to dance! You can dance in Islamiyat class!

ZAYA: No . . .

MAULANA: Arey, I don't lie, beta! You know this, dancing is not bad. There is time aur place for dancing, samjhe?

Beat.

You know this, I see how good are you. I see it now. Not before. Before you just okay. But some thing take time to be good, aur now I see it inside you. What's in there, huh, what's in there? Pure shiny gold istar. Hmm. Beta, you are most improvement. You listen so good good now.

ZAYA: Thank you.

MAULANA: If you keep it up, I give you shiny cricket bat on Eid.

ZAYA: Oh. Uh. No thanks.

MAULANA: Arey! How you say no thanks to very ispecial gift? You must earn anyway! I don't just give you, okay! Chalo. Earn it.

Beat.

Open your mouth.

ZAYA: What?

MAULANA: Open your mouth, beta, aur repeat me! Chalo! Allah'huminey.

Beat.

ZAYA: Allah'huminey.

MAULANA: Allah kasam tho.

ZAYA: Allah kasam tho.

MAULANA: Wabey ka aman tho.

ZAYA: Wabey ka aman tho.

MAULANA: Walaika thava kal tho.

ZAYA: Walaika . . .

MAULANA: Thava / kal tho.

ZAYA: Thava kal tho.

MAULANA: Good boy!

MAULANA takes ZAYA's hand and spins him.

Wa'ala riskay ka . . .

ZAYA: Wa'ala riskay ka!

Spins again.

MAULANA: Aftaar tho!

ZAYA: Aftaar tho!

Spins again. ZAYA laughs.

MAULANA: Fun, hai na?

ZAYA: Yeah . . .

MAULANA: Chalo jao, mummy ko bathao ke you know opening fast prayer now tho you are ready to istart fasting!!

ZAYA: Okay!

MAULANA: Aur beta, say her ke it's okay some thing take time to be good!

ZAYA: Okay!

MAULANA: Aur beta, don't say her ke you can dance in my Islamiyat class. This is top isecret. Chalo jao, go to mummy!

MAULANA spins ZAYA one final time, then gently pushes him towards MA. ZAYA enters her hospital room once again. This time, MA stands, wearing the shalwar kameez SALIM brought her. They just look at each other for a beat.

ZAYA: That shalwar kameez looks nice on you.

MA: Meh ne socha ke you left.

ZAYA: No. I'm still . . . I can't stay here though.

MA: Laila aarahi hai?

ZAYA: Yeah, she'll be here really soon. She'll wait with you until the doctor can give you an update, and then she'll take you home, okay?

MA: Meh salon jaongi.

ZAYA: But—

Beat.

How are you doing?

MA: Meh teekh hoon.

A little silence.

ZAYA: Ma—

MA: Teekh hai.

ZAYA: No wait, Ma, I . . . I'm sorry about what I said to you.

A little more silence. MA *picks up the gift box and offers it to* ZAYA.

MA: Yeh leyna hai?

ZAYA: No, thanks, Ma. I'm—I'm fasting today.

MA: Aaj? Kyun?

ZAYA: Salim asked me to.

Beat.

MA: Acha teekh hai. Chalo, ab Eid pey mujhe visit karo, acha?

ZAYA: Okay. Yeah, okay.

MA: You want to go to Mubeen's wedding?

ZAYA: No.

MA: Teekh hai. Ab tum ja sakte ho.

ZAYA *doesn't leave.*

Zaya?

ZAYA: Ma . . . Can I ask you something?

Beat.

Do you think I'm good? Do you think I'm a good person?

A silence.

MA: Meh sochthi hoon ke . . . We come to this world good. Tum mera beta ho. I bring you here. Likhen, tumhara marzi hai—you choose to stay good. If you want.

Another silence.

ZAYA: Okay. I'm going.

MA: Acha, allah'hafiz, beta.

ZAYA: Allah'hafiz, Ma.

ZAYA starts to leave.

MA: Zaya?

ZAYA turns around.

Yeh . . . Salim ko dey do. Iftaari mein kao.

> *MA looks down as she extends the gift box of sweets to ZAYA again. ZAYA is taken by this gesture, even as MA tries to downplay it. ZAYA manages to take the gift box and then leaves, still processing. He doesn't know exactly where he is going. MUBEEN suddenly follows behind, carrying a cricket bat. It is different than the one he had before.*

MUBEEN: Eh! Stop. Where you think you going, man?!

ZAYA: Leave me alone.

MUBEEN: Woooow, guy, that's how you gonna talk to your childhood buddy after like ten years of not speaking, brah?? That's coooold!

ZAYA turns around.

ZAYA: Hi. I don't feel like talking to you right now.

MUBEEN: Come on, man, long time no see!!

ZAYA: Okay. Why are you doing here?

MUBEEN: What?

ZAYA: What do you want from me?

MUBEEN: What you want?

ZAYA: Nothing.

MUBEEN: You sure?

MUBEEN takes a step back from ZAYA.

Eh eh, just so you know, I whip over here on Fridays cuz I don't got uni and I like to party in Sauga. Damn, shit's poppin' here—nothing going on in fucking Bitchener! And, guy, guyyy, your school's so lax too, so many brownies I walk right in and they don't even know I don't even go here, brah!! Fucking sick!

ZAYA: Mubeen, I can't really do this right now.

MUBEEN: Can't really do what, man—we just catching up. Chill—fucking breathe! Eh eh, I gotta ask you—you seen me? You seen me and Junaid and Adeel, right, in the prayer room standing in the back, not even praying, just watching Sadiya and her slutty-ass friends bending over for me like—

MUBEEN brings his hands to his ears then bends over as Sadiya perhaps would.

La'ilaha'illala motherfucka!

MUBEEN laughs.

You seen that, right?

ZAYA: No . . .

MUBEEN: Really?

Beat.

Bro, where you tryna go right now? Home?

ZAYA nods.

Where's that? Ahhh yeah, you still living in those shitty apartments, right.
I think I remember where that is. Lemme give you a ride.

ZAYA: No thanks.

MUBEEN: Damn, you cold and stupid and still lying too, eh? When you
ever gonna learn?

ZAYA: What?

MUBEEN: You saying you don't watch me in the prayer room, but how
come Adeel saying you are?

ZAYA: I'm—not.

MUBEEN: Man, Adeel still goes here. He seen you walking up and down
the prayer room hallway every fucking Friday afternoon, even when I'm
not there, so like what is that, eh? You looking for me, bro?

ZAYA: No . . .

MUBEEN: Got something to ask me? Wanna know how I'm doing? Wanna know how your maulana saab is doing? Still teaching those Islamiyat classes? Giving out gold stars and cricket bats? Eh? You wanna know, guy? Go ahead. Ask me what you want from me.

ZAYA: I don't want anything from you.

MUBEEN: All right, man, that's cool, that's cool. Only problem is, Adeel's thinking it's fucking creepy how you always tryna watch me, so he told me to take care of it.

MUBEEN slowly approaches ZAYA, swinging his bat. ZAYA is stuck.

ZAYA: I'm just . . . trying to go home.

MUBEEN: Yeah, I don't think so. Get down.

ZAYA: What? No.

MUBEEN: Get on your fucking knees.

ZAYA: Mubeen, I swear I don't want anything from you. I'm sorry, / I'm sorry I watched you.

MUBEEN: Shut the fuck up.

ZAYA looks around.

ZAYA: Mubeen, can we please—uh, just do this, um, somewhere else?

MUBEEN: On your knees, bitch. Now.

MUBEEN leans towards ZAYA. ZAYA gets on his knees.

Good. Now put it in your mouth.

MUBEEN takes a step back and brings the handle of the cricket bat to ZAYA's mouth. ZAYA looks at MUBEEN.

Put it in your mouth.

ZAYA hesitates, then does so. He sucks on the handle of the cricket bat while MUBEEN looks down at him. This goes on in silence.

Good. Now get up.

ZAYA gets up.

Good.

Beat.

Now hit me. Hit me.

ZAYA hesitates, then tries to shove MUBEEN.

Don't touch me like a fucking khusra. I said hit me.

ZAYA slaps MUBEEN across the face, hard.

Good.

Beat.

Now hit me with this.

MUBEEN motions with the cricket bat.

ZAYA: No. I won't do that.

MUBEEN shoves the cricket bat in ZAYA's hands.

MUBEEN: HIT ME. HIT ME. HIT ME.

ZAYA hesitates. And then he strikes MUBEEN in the head with the cricket bat. MUBEEN falls down. ZAYA tries to run away, but it's like he's going nowhere. It's like time is frozen, but at the same time ZAYA can see the sun is going down.

He blinks. He can't believe his eyes. He panics. When he turns, somehow he finds himself at home. He sees SALIM, who is in the middle of praying. Their luggage and a pair of heels sit close by. There is a container of food near the luggage. ZAYA watches SALIM.

SALIM moves out of the sajhda position (hands, knees and forehead to the ground) into sitting on their heels and knees, relaxed back. Beat. They go back into sajhda and then back into their sitting position. They pray internally here for a while.

They raise their right index finger briefly and then lower it. They continue to pray. Upon finishing, they slowly look to the right, hold a soft gaze, then slowly look to the left, holding again.

They sit in a more relaxed position now, bringing their cupped hands just in front of their chest, praying into their hands. When finished, they wash over their face with their hands.

ZAYA waits until SALIM is done praying before speaking. SALIM starts to pack away their ja-namaz.

ZAYA: Salim, I . . .

SALIM: Mujhe nahi suna hai. You said you'd be home by three. It's after eight. I waited for you.

ZAYA: I—I just lost track of time and . . .

SALIM: I wasn't sure if I was going to see you before I go.

ZAYA: I'm sorry. The GO bus got delayed / I think . . .

SALIM: Zaya, we spent the whole day apart. Aur ab meh ja rahi hoon.

ZAYA: I'm really sorry. I don't know what else to say. Let me, uh, let me—can I—can I hold you?

SALIM: No.

ZAYA: Please.

SALIM: I don't want you to touch me right now.

　　Beat.

ZAYA: When do you have to go? I can call us a ride.

SALIM: Meri taxi aarahi hai.

ZAYA: Okay, okay, well we still have some time together. I'm gonna wait with you at the airport.

SALIM: No.

ZAYA: What? Salim, don't do this to me. Please, please forgive me before you go. Wait. Actually—please don't leave.

SALIM: My flight's in three hours, Zaya.

ZAYA: Don't go.

SALIM: What?

ZAYA: Stay. With me. Please.

SALIM: Kyun? Why would I do that? This is my Umrah trip. I'm going to Mecca with my mom, yeh mere liye bahot important hai aur you don't want me to go?

ZAYA: No, of course I do, sorry.

SALIM: I'm leaving, Zaya. Aur mujhe nahi patha ke meh kab wapas aarahi hoon.

ZAYA: What do you mean?

SALIM: Mere paas return ticket nahi hai.

ZAYA: Yeah, because you said your ma's gonna buy it for you when you get there. Right? You have to come back before the summer ends. You have your teaching job in the fall.

SALIM: I sent in a request for an extended personal leave.

ZAYA: What? When?

SALIM: Earlier today.

ZAYA: When?

SALIM: When I got home masjid ke baad.

ZAYA: Salim, that's a really impulsive fucking thing to do.

SALIM: It's not. I've been thinking about it for a little while.

ZAYA: But you never told me. Why would you do this to me?

SALIM: Zaya.

ZAYA: Why wouldn't you just tell me?

SALIM: There's nothing really to say, Zaya. We haven't been talking. Aur meh—meh nahi pretend kar sakti hoon ke I don'tknow who you are anymore or what you're going through. I don't know. Tum mujhe nahi batha thay ho. You don't let me in. Aur meh koshish karti hoon to really be here for you but you don't—you don't let me love you. So, hum kya kar rahey hain?

ZAYA: I don't know! But if you leave right now we won't be able to figure this out together.

SALIM: This—isn't working. It hasn't been working. I haven't been feeling anything. Have you?

ZAYA doesn't respond right away. SALIM starts putting on their heels.

ZAYA: Salim, okay, I know I fucked up today. I wasn't good today. I haven't been good to you, I know—I'll change. I can be good. Salim, I'm sorry. I'll do anything for you. I promise.

SALIM: I don't want you to do anything. Mujhe kuch nahi chahiye tumse.

A little silence.

Have you opened your fast yet?

ZAYA: No.

SALIM: I made seekh kabob rolls. I kind of burnt them. I left the rest in the fridge, but I held onto these in case you'd come home. They're still warm. And not as burnt.

SALIM gives the container of food to ZAYA.

ZAYA: Hey . . . I didn't break my fast today. Can you believe that?

Beat.

And look, look, Salim, Ma gave this to you. She said to me—she said, "Give this to Salim."

ZAYA holds out the gift box of sweets. SALIM *takes it. It means a lot to* SALIM *that* MA *made this gesture, but they try to contain what they are feeling. Then their phone rings. Their taxi is here.*

SALIM: Mujhe jaana hai, Zaya. Allah'hafiz.

ZAYA: Salim . . . Please . . .

SALIM takes their luggage and leaves.

Wait wait wait. Please don't leave me here alone! Oh god . . .

ZAYA looks around. Emptiness. He looks down at the container of food. He opens it. He takes out a seekh kabob roll and begins to eat it. Silence.

ZAYA can't eat. He throws his wrap on the ground and falls over. He curls into a ball. It's as if he's throwing a tantrum.

Then MA *appears in a different, fancier shalwar kameez, carrying a purse and wearing a little bit of jewellery.*

MA: Beta? Kya ho raha hai? Big Eid party in one hour aur tum aise . . .

ZAYA: Mummy!

ZAYA throws himself onto MA. He clings onto her and pulls her to the ground.

MA: Beta kya kar rahey—

MA sees the wrap on the ground.

Arey Allah! Zaya yeh khana zameen pey kyun hai? Oh ho, Zaya, yeh bahothi buri baat hai!

MA takes out some napkins from her purse and cleans up the mess. She puts the wrap back into the container and puts it in her purse.

Zaya, kya soch rahey thay? If someone else see you . . . We are guest here, beta!

ZAYA holds really tightly onto MA.

Arey! Yeh kya pagalpan hai?

ZAYA: Mummy Mummy . . . I just don't feel good . . .

MA: Likhen kya ho gaya tumko?? Zaya, agar yeh excuse hai—

ZAYA: It's not, Mummy, CAN YOU JUST BELIEVE ME I don't feel good! I just—I just wanna feel good . . .

MA: Tho meh kya kar sakti hoon?

ZAYA: What's in your purse?

MA: No! No more seekh kabob roll.

ZAYA: Nail polish?

MA: Likhen mere nails done hai.

ZAYA: Paint my nails. Right now.

MA: Zaya . . .

ZAYA: What? You do it for all your clients at the salon. So my turn.

MA: Beta, nahi. You be so good this month, so much improvement aur aaj, Eid ka din, tum aise behave kar rahey ho? Kyun?

ZAYA: I don't feel good and I wanna feel good right now! Paint my nails or else I'm gonna CRY and SUCK MY THUMB and DANCE and—

MA: Beta, awaaz neechey.

ZAYA: AND I'LL SCREAM!

MA: Acha acha, ek minute, beta!

MA sets down her purse and rummages through it looking for some nail polish.

ZAYA: Come on, come on, come on, I need to feel GOOD!

MA finds some nail polish and quickly begins to paint his nails.

Make me feel good! YES!

MA: Zaya, party se pehle you have to remove this. Samjhe?

ZAYA: Oh wow, I feel so good, Mummy, thank you!!

MA hasn't finished painting one hand before ZAYA throws his arms around her and hugs her.

You're the best, Mummy!

MA: Okay, okay, beta.

ZAYA caresses MA. He nuzzles his head in her chest. He doesn't want to let go. MA begins to feel uncomfortable.

Okay, beta . . .

ZAYA doesn't let go. MA tries to gently push him off. She struggles.

Beta, kya kar rahey ho? Chodho mujhe!

MAULANA's voice is heard in the distance.

MAULANA: *(from off)* Zaya! Beta! Kahan ho?

MA: Zaya! Maulana saab aarahey hain!

ZAYA: Wait, Mummy, just a little bit longer . . .

MA: Zaya, tumhare nakhun!

MA pushes ZAYA away.

Put your hands in your pocket.

MA stuffs ZAYA's hands in his own pockets.

Bahar mat nikhalo.

MA puts away the nail polish and barely manages to cover her head with her scarf. ZAYA straightens up just as MAULANA appears, hands behind his back.

MAULANA: Ah, begum! Eid Mubarak.

MA: Eid Mubarak, maulana saab.

MAULANA: Eid Mubarak, beta.

ZAYA: Eid Mubarak!

MAULANA: Beta, I have ispecial surprise for you on this beautiful Eid day. Dekhna hai?

MA: Oh maulana saab, shayad iftaari ke baad? Zaya ko . . . washroom jaana hai, hai na?

ZAYA: Yes . . .

MAULANA: Likhen beta, you don't want to see this very ispecial gift?

MA: Maulana saab, bahot shukriya likhen—

MAULANA: Dekho! Yeh aapke liye, for being iso pure most shiny gold istar boy!

MAULANA holds out the cricket bat that was once given to MUBEEN. MA takes it.

MA: Vah so nice!

MAULANA: Begum, yeh aapka beta ke liye.

MAULANA takes the cricket bat back and gives it to ZAYA, who takes it by the handle with his unpainted hand.

ZAYA: Oh. Thank you.

MAULANA: Nice, hai na?

ZAYA: Yeah.

MAULANA: Iswing it. You can iswing it!

MA: Maulana saab, yeh sab iftaari ke baad ho sakta—

MAULANA: Begum, actually meh Zaya se baat karna chatha hoon one-to-one. Sirf one minute ke liye.

MA: Oh. Haan. Bilkul. Bilkul.

MA points to a corner of the room.

Meh wahan wait kar sakti hoon?

MAULANA: Upistair, please.

MA: Haan, bilkul.

(to ZAYA) Be good. I am right here.

MA leaves.

MAULANA: Acha chalo, swing karo!

ZAYA tries to swing with one hand holding the bat, but it's pretty heavy.

Oh ho, beta, you must swing with both hand!

MAULANA takes ZAYA's other hand out of his pocket and sees the painted nails. He freezes.

ZAYA: What? What happened? What happened now? Didn't you . . . Didn't you look at my nails and say cute?

MAULANA: Cute.

ZAYA: No no, you said pretty. No no no, you said beautiful. You called them beautiful.

MAULANA: Beautiful.

ZAYA: And then you walked away.

MAULANA starts to walk away.

Then you turned around and said—

ZAYA & MAULANA: See you at the Eid party.

ZAYA: Then you left, right? Wait, no. That can't be it. You, you closed down the masjid after this. After the party. The next day you closed down. Did something happen at the party? No, no, we couldn't talk to each other because . . . You were with all the uncles all night and I kept trying to distract Sadiya from Mubeen, even though the boys weren't allowed to be with the girls. I remember. I remember that. It happened here. Right now. Something happened here before you left. Come back.

MAULANA comes back.

You looked at my nails and you called them—

ZAYA & MAULANA: Beautiful.

ZAYA: Then you kissed my hand. No wait, you didn't. You spun me around.

MAULANA spins ZAYA.

Three times.

MAULANA spins ZAYA two more times.

Then you said . . .

ZAYA & MAULANA: You want to dance a little?

ZAYA: No, fuck, wait—in Urdu!

ZAYA & MAULANA: Thoda sa nachna hai?

ZAYA: You sat down. Right there. You sat down and you . . . watched me. I danced. Around the cricket bat. There was Bollywood music.

MAULANA sits down. Bollywood music plays.

Loud. Louder!

Bollywood music blares.

And I danced. Like this. No, no, like this! Like this. And you said—

ZAYA & MAULANA: Hot? You are hot? Pant uthar do.

ZAYA: It was summer. August. June. I don't know. I took off my pants like this.

ZAYA takes off his pants.

You watched me. I kept dancing. The music was so good. Fuck! Fuck you, Madhuri Dixit! Madhuri fucking Dick-Shit!!!

ZAYA laughs.

Yeah, yeah yeah yeah, I laughed—I laughed because this couldn't be real . . . you said—

ZAYA & MAULANA: You can put it in your mouth if you want.

ZAYA: Okay! So I did!

ZAYA puts his thumb in his mouth and dances around.

AND I KEPT FUCKING DANCING! And you must've thought it was so fucking hot cuz you . . . yeah you . . . you started to . . .

MAULANA starts to jerk off.

Yeah, yeah, you started to . . . And I stood there, with my thumb in my mouth, watching you. You watched me and I watched you. Ma was waiting upstairs. You said you wanted to talk to me for a minute and it took way longer than a fucking minute.

Beat.

And then you . . .

MAULANA freezes.

Come. Come. You came, didn't you? Come right now. I want you to come right now. Isn't that what happened, maulana saab? You came and you felt so gross after, so you shut down the masjid. Right? You came right in front of your pure shiny gold star boy. Right? Why did you stop? Is this it? Is this all that happened? No!

Come. Come. Come! COME! COOOOOME!

Nothing.

OH FUCK THIS! YOU'RE NOT EVEN FUCKING REAL, MAULANA SAAB.

MAULANA leaves.

No no no, wait, don't go don't go. Come back! Please?

Beat. ZAYA *realizes what he just said. He takes a moment to breathe. Then he quickly puts on his pants. He chooses to pick up the cricket bat. And as he comes to stand,* MUBEEN *appears before him.*

Hi. Mubeen.

MUBEEN: Zaya . . .

ZAYA: How are you?

MUBEEN: I'm . . . okay. Oh hey, is that my old cricket bat?

ZAYA: Yes. This is yours. I'm returning it.

MUBEEN: Okay so, are you gonna give it . . . to me?

ZAYA: Oh. Yes. Sorry. Here.

ZAYA gives the bat to MUBEEN.

MUBEEN: Man, I used to love this thing. Yeah, and the gold stars down the . . . Thanks. Uh. So, welcome to Kitchener.

ZAYA: Thanks. Um . . . Sorry for dropping by so late.

MUBEEN: It's okay. You wanna sit?

ZAYA: No, I should actually . . . You know, I came here pretty impulsively and so I should . . . I mean, I'm realizing that this wasn't the—okay. Basically, I thought I wanted to talk to your father, but I don't want to do that anymore. Thank you for taking the cricket bat.

MUBEEN: Zaya . . . He, he's actually not doing well. Not sure if your amma told you or anything, but his health has just been slowly declining these last few months. He just stays in his room mostly now. He sleeps a lot, doesn't do much . . .

ZAYA: Oh.

MUBEEN: He's not gonna come out. It's okay if you wanna sit and talk for a bit. I can make us some chai. Sorry I don't have any alcohol.

ZAYA: It's pretty late. Thank you though.

MUBEEN: What were you gonna say to him?

ZAYA: What?

MUBEEN: What did you want to say to my abba?

ZAYA: I don't know. I just . . . I want to know why he closed down the masjid . . . Do you know? It was twenty years ago, I know, but . . .

MUBEEN: I, uh, I'm not sure . . .

ZAYA: My ma said it was my fault.

MUBEEN: Oh. I don't know what she's talking about.

A little silence.

ZAYA: What about the Eid party? Just before the masjid closed? Do you remember anything about that night?

MUBEEN: Zaya, I don't know. I—don't really think about it.

ZAYA: Can you try?

MUBEEN: I—I think I remember Abba was really quiet after the party ended. I thought that was—not like him.

ZAYA: He was really quiet?

MUBEEN: Yeah.

ZAYA: Did he tell you why?

MUBEEN: No . . .

ZAYA: What else do you remember? About the Eid party?

MUBEEN: I remember seeing you with this.

MUBEEN *refers to the cricket bat.*

And I remember feeling . . . jealous.

ZAYA: Did you . . . did you tell him what we used to do together? Like kissing and—

MUBEEN: Zaya, I don't—I can't remember.

ZAYA: You don't remember telling your dad something like that?

MUBEEN: I don't know.

ZAYA: You don't know what?

MUBEEN: Zaya, honestly, I just don't like to think about my childhood a lot, okay?

ZAYA: Why not?

MUBEEN: It's hard for me. A lot of stuff happened that you don't know about. At a certain point, a long time ago, I just stopped asking questions. Or even wondered things. I just—stopped. And look, I don't know why the masjid closed down. I don't know why we moved. He didn't tell me those things. I never asked. But . . . I always thought he did something to you. I don't know what, but he did something. And I thought maybe that night, the one you're asking about, he did something really bad to you. I don't know. That's what I can remember. Honestly.

A silence.

ZAYA: Okay.

MUBEEN: I just, I'm trying to—things are changing in my life and I'm just trying to—be honest. With myself.

Beat.

Sadiya's calling off the wedding. So . . . I was just dropping off the gift box as a formality. We'll tell all the aunties after Eid so they don't talk shit about us on Eid.

ZAYA: Oh, shit.

MUBEEN: If you're feeling sorry, don't. It's a good decision. Makes sense. Uh, anyways . . . Thanks for returning my cricket bat.

Beat.

Ever learn how to properly swing it?

ZAYA shakes his head.

Wanna learn?

ZAYA: Not really, no.

MUBEEN: You sure? It's a lot of fun.

ZAYA: I'm sure it is.

MUBEEN swings the bat.

MUBEEN: Woohoo!

ZAYA: Wow, you look like you're having a lot of fun.

MUBEEN: I am.

A silence.

ZAYA: Okay. I have to go.

MUBEEN: Okay.

ZAYA walks away. He finds some light and sits down in it. After a moment SALIM slowly emerges and joins him.

ZAYA: Wow. Hey.

SALIM: Hello.

ZAYA: I know you're not actually here . . .

SALIM shrugs their shoulders, smiles.

You really don't know if you're coming back?

SALIM: I just need time to . . . think.

ZAYA: You don't have a plan?

SALIM: I mean, not really. Well, mujhe patha hai ke meh Eid Dubai mein celebrate kar rahi hoon with Mom. And then right after that we're going to Mecca, and from there we might actually go somewhere in Africa or back to Dubai or . . . Humko nahi patha. We're still dreaming.

Beat.

My dad might be able to set me up with a teaching job in Pakistan, but I'll only take it if they let me wear my bra to class.

ZAYA: Seriously?

SALIM: Under all my clothes, of course. I'll layer nicely. Fikar nahi karo.

ZAYA: Salim . . .

SALIM: I told my mom I'd like to wear my bra while we do Umrah and she thinks it's a great idea.

ZAYA: Okay, I don't know if you're just fucking with me now or . . .

SALIM: I'm not. This is what I want.

Beat.

ZAYA: Hey. I hope you take good care of yourself, okay?

SALIM: Aap bhi kayal rakhna. Please. Sleep. And stop watching *Koffee with Karan.*

ZAYA: Okay.

ZAYA and SALIM laugh together. Then a long silence follows.

Salim, I'm, I'm sorry I hurt you. I'm sorry I pushed you away from me. I just, I never wanted you to leave me and I didn't know how to tell you that. I kept pushing you because I kept telling myself I didn't deserve anything good. And I've been doing this to myself for a really long time because, um, something happened to me when I was young and it's . . . Still with me. Because I've never really talked about it. But I'd like to tell you about it. And I know when we were together I didn't tell you a lot of things, but I want to—I want to tell you everything now. I want to say things I've been, like, screaming inside to say to you for years. It doesn't matter if it's too late, I, I—meh aapse pyaar karta hoon.

A little silence.

SALIM: I love you too, pyaare. Mujhe sab kuch bathao.

ZAYA and SALIM sit together in the light. SALIM slowly rests their hand on top of ZAYA's. ZAYA closes his eyes.

GLOSSARY

In an effort to centre readers who understand the language, no Urdu dialogue is translated in this book. Instead, you will find here a list of some specific cultural moments or references throughout the play that are unpacked/explained because they have deeper meanings than what Google may be able to tell you.

Page 4   *Aaja Nachle*

A Bollywood film released in 2007 starring Madhuri Dixit (who is referenced later in the play as well). The film marked Madhuri's "comeback" to cinema after taking a five-year hiatus. Though dancing is heavily featured in many Bollywood films, *Aaja Nachle* is one that explores the vitality of dance in and among community.

Page 5   "Today's the last Friday before Eid"

The Qur'an denotes Friday as a sacred day of worship for all practising Muslims. The last Friday before Eid is regarded by some Muslims as one of the most important days of the year.

Page 16   surah falaq

There are 114 surahs (or chapters) in the Qur'an. This surah in particular is about seeking refuge from evil, darkness and malignant witchcraft.

Page 17   Stepping on ja-namaz with no intention to pray

Culturally, this is frowned upon. It is understood that when your feet
make contact with the ja-namaz, you have made the commitment to pray.
So when this is not the case, it is seen as a disrespectful act.

Page 29   "Yeh shirt-pant ley kar aa—um, is that okay?"

In this moment, Salim was about to conjugate the verb "aaye" in the feminine tense in Urdu. This is something they always do when referring to
themself in Urdu. They cut themself off and switch to English because
they are in the presence of Ma.

Page 46   "Meh kuch kar—meh kuch kar sakti hoon?"

In this moment, Salim cuts themself off again as they were about to conjugate another verb into the feminine tense in Urdu, in front of Ma. But
this time, they choose to go ahead with it in the feminine tense as they
speak their following line in Urdu. They do this knowing it is something
both Ma and Zaya will hear.

Though the journey from first draft to book publication was seven years in total, it feels apt to claim I started writing *Acha Bacha* at a very young age in my life. For almost as long as I can remember, I was collecting moments I witnessed in my parents' home and in the world and storing them in my brain for no reason in particular. Certainly never with the intention to one day write out these collected moments. Never, because, also at a very young age, I began internalizing messaging from the world and from within my parents' home that the stories that lived in my head were not worth taking up space elsewhere.

No one cares about what I have to say. No one will understand what I have to say.

By the time I started high school, I made peace with this messaging. And, despite that, I started writing plays because I needed to process certain feelings I felt I couldn't talk about directly with people. Feelings of shame, of unworthiness, of being unlovable. I kept writing, and even shared my work publicly again and again, because I told myself: none of this really matters because it will never amount to anything anyways. Also, it was just high school.

In grade ten, I remember reading *White Biting Dog* by Judith Thompson. I remember it being the first time I ever felt anything while reading anything. I remember being so taken by this feeling of finally feeling while reading. I remember dreaming about writing a play and having it published one day, so that maybe I could make other people feel things while reading. I remember dreaming about the endless possibilities of fonts that could be used to spell out my name on the front cover of the book. I remember these dreams feeling so impossible, but I loved it anyways.

By June 2012, at the end of high school, I was convinced by my drama teachers—Wendie Gibbons and Nikolette Savic—that pursuing theatre post-secondary could actually be a possibility for me. I didn't know that before. My writer's craft teacher, Don MacDougall, called me a "big fish in a little pond," and even though in the moment I didn't believe him, I knew I'd never forget him saying that to me.

Less than a year later, I submitted the very first draft of *Acha Bacha* to Judith Thompson as one of her playwriting students at the University of Guelph. I had never written South Asian characters, nor in Urdu prior to Judith's class. Her magic stirred, unlocked, awakened stories and voices I didn't know I was allowed to share with the world. This was exhilarating.

In the summer of 2013 I met Damien Atkins. The immense respect and care I felt from Damien—not only about my work but about who I was as a person—sparked a belief in myself that felt so foreign at the time. Damien saw a light in me that I convinced myself was diminishing due to personal stuff I was contending with while trying to write my play. And at the same time, Damien's fierce and uncompromising generosity filled me with hope—a tremendous gift I needed to keep me going.

Through the spring of 2014, I was a playwright-in-residence at the Paprika Festival, where I received dramaturgy on *Acha Bacha* from Djanet Sears. If it weren't for Djanet speaking about the power of two people from the same cultural background falling in love with each other, the character of Salim may have remained a cis white guy (as they were initially conceived . . . I know, I can't believe it either). Dan Daley committed to securing South Asian, Urdu-speaking actors for the workshop and presentation of the work and saw that commitment all the way through. This told me that the dreams I thought I buried were allowed to come true. More possibilities began to unlock in my head. I started to think about what a production of this play might look like, and how the rehearsal process might unfold. The world started to shift.

If it weren't for the platform Paprika gave me, I wouldn't have had the opportunity to share the work in development publicly. At the staged reading, Andy McKim began the conversation with me about having the play continue its development journey with Theatre Passe Muraille. By the spring of 2016, with TPM's support, I had received a $10,000 playwriting grant from the Ontario Arts Council, which effectively pulled me out of the overdraft my bank account was sitting in.

As months passed, not only did it feel that my play was morphing and growing up, but that I too was morphing and growing up. I was feeling strong. I became clearer and clearer on who I was as an artist and what I wanted to say. And the provocation that lived so deep inside *Acha Bacha* was so clear too: let's see what happens when we put queer/trans and South Asian people so authentically and unapologetically at the centre of this theatrical experience.

Let's see what happens when we say "I care about you and I understand you" in our work to people who may not always feel cared for or understood in our world.

And at the beginning of 2018, rehearsals began. The process I had dreamt about for years now—one that was full of respect and kindness and making so much space for all the artists of colour involved—never had a shot at materializing because the very little whiteness that was invited into the room managed to centre itself quite early on in the process. It came along with a severe colonial rigidity that only pushed my play further away from what it wanted to be. And as negative things were said out loud in the rehearsal room about the designers' work (who were predominantly women of colour), the actors work (who were all people of colour) and about my work as a playwright, I started to feel myself shrink. Like, really shrink. Like, smaller than the child collecting life moments in their mind but never writing them down.

As the process spiralled downwards, I was tasked with rewriting major chunks of the play on a daily basis while being expected to attend as much rehearsal as possible. I lost so much sleep over two weeks and really wasn't eating well. The image of the "strong artist" I felt I was becoming evaporated in days. I tried to find every reason to get out of that rehearsal room. Thankfully, my playwright fee was so low I had good reason in leaving to maintain my joe job at the time.

I needed to get out because I couldn't believe I was letting white supremacy crush me. I couldn't stand another one of his speeches—to a room with almost all people of colour—where he went on and on about how he felt he was the only one doing work on the project. I couldn't stand being told a few days before opening that my script was "never ready." I couldn't stand making any more space for his attitude, his tantrums, his freak-outs, his harsh words, his claim that no one would understand my play.

On opening night, as I watched the play unfold, I distinctly remember sitting with friends and loved ones thinking, "This is not the play I set out to write." I could hear how the whiteness stifled the characters I had spent five years really getting to know and love. The dream of how this work was supposed to come into this world was destroyed. And I couldn't help but tell myself perhaps it was never meant to be anyways.

Then the love poured in. And I could feel it. Queer and trans South Asians showed up to the run in numbers. They entered a space—a historically white space—and took their seats to experience a work that wanted so badly to put them at the centre. A Colour Deep, a community-based organization, brought over twenty queer/trans South Asian folks to one of the previews. People shared with me how they felt seen in the work, how they saw their mothers in the work, how their entire lives were reflected in the work. People travelled two hours or more to get from where they were in the GTA to the theatre. Audience members came back more than once. A debrief space was held for QTBIPOC communities after one of the performances so we could have an honest conversation on what the work stirred in us. People, South Asian and beyond, not only understood the play, but they felt things.

My deepest gratitude to Ellora, Qasim, Matt, Omar, Erum, Tijiki, Joanna, C.J., Kat, Dirk, Sidrah, Anu, kumari, Berkha, Yami, Harris, Harmeet and Angel for keeping me buoyed by sharing your love with me during the rehearsal process and production run.

A few months after closing, the play was swiftly translated into French by Olivier Sylvestre through the Glassco Translation Residency in Tadoussac, Quebec. This opportunity gave me the chance to dive quickly back into the work and rewrite the parts that I felt I really didn't even write. And eat lobster for the first time ever in my life at the beautiful home we stayed in.

And in the months leading up to the publication of this book, I have been so thorough in picking apart every moment of this play to ensure it no longer wreaks of white supremacy. To ensure that the play returned back to its roots of centring queer/trans South Asians in its storytelling. To ensure that this whole book is nothing but honest, authentic and unapologetic. A complete honouring of the journey of losing your voice somewhere unknowingly, then reverting to believing perhaps it never mattered anyways, so who cares, and finally speaking truth, even if it's too late. Thank you to Playwrights Canada Press (Annie, Blake and Jessica) for making this space for me. For putting my name on a book cover. For letting the words be exactly what they are.

And finally, to the people who were there every step of the way, my siblings: Babar and Arsal. Thank you for caring for me. Thank you for understanding me. Always.

—Bilal Baig
July 2020

Bilal Baig (they/them) is a queer trans-feminine Muslim playwright and workshop facilitator. Bilal's plays include *Kitne Saare Laloo Yahan Pey Hain*, *Kainchee Lagaa*, and *Acha Bacha*. Bilal is a workshop facilitator for non-profits such as Story Planet and Rivers of Hope Collective, and was a founding member of acolourdeep.ca, a platform that strives to create online/offline spaces for queer/trans South Asians across the GTA. Bilal is based in Toronto.

First edition: July 2020
Printed and bound in Canada by Rapido Books, Montreal

Jacket art and design by Harmeet Rehal
Author photo © Greg Wong

**PLAYWRIGHTS
CANADA PRESS**
202-269 Richmond St. W.
Toronto, ON
M5V 1X1

416.703.0013
info@playwrightscanada.com
www.playwrightscanada.com
@playcanpress